KET
Practice Tests

1

STUDENT'S BOOK

Susan McGeary

Richmond PUBLISHING

Richmond Publishing
19 Berghem Mews
Blythe Road
London W14 OHN

© Susan McGeary 1995

First published by Richmond Publishing® 1995
Reprinted 1996

ISBN: 84–294–4665–6

Author's Acknowledgement

Thanks to Min for typing the manuscript and to my mother
for researching signs in England.

Printed in Spain by Gráfica Internacional, S.A.

D.L.: M-22.347-1997

315138

CONTENTS

TEST 1   FAMILY

READING AND WRITING PAPER

Part 1
Questions 1 – 5

Who are these notices for?
For questions 1 – 5, mark A, B or C.

EXAMPLE		ANSWER
0 DANGER CHILDREN CROSSING	A drivers B children C mothers	A

1 **PLEASE PARK AT THE BACK**

A drivers

B students

C conductors

2 BEWARE OF THE DOG

A dog owners

B people in a restaurant

C everybody

3 *PLEASE CLOSE THE GATE*

A shoppers

B passengers

C campers

4 **NO SMOKING**

A drivers

B customers

C housewives

5 **Children playing – Be Careful**

A families

B housewives

C drivers

Questions 6 – 10

Which notice (A – H) says this (6 – 10)?
For questions 6 – 10, mark the correct letter (A – H).

EXAMPLE	ANSWER
0 Don't wait.	E

6   We won't be long.

7   Your meal is in the cooker.

8   John will telephone again.

9   Take dishes out of dishwasher.

10   Give the dog something to eat.

A   Lunch in oven

B   Put dishes into dishwasher

C   BACK SOON

D   John rang again, you have to phone him back

E   We won't be back for a long time

F   John phoned, will ring back later

G   Feed Bruno

H   Empty dishwasher please

Part 2
Questions 11 – 15

Read the descriptions (11 – 15) of some rooms in a house.
What is the name of each place (A – H)?
For questions 11 – 15, mark the correct letter (A – H).

EXAMPLE	ANSWER
0 You eat here.	H

11   You sleep here.

12   You wash yourself here.

13   You make meals here.

14   You read and watch TV here.

15   You park your car here.

ROOMS

A   study

B   bedroom

C   garage

D   bathroom

E   hall

F   living room

G   kitchen

H   dining room

Part 3
Questions 16 – 20

Complete the five conversations.
For questions 16 – 20, mark A, B or C.

EXAMPLE		ANSWER
0 How many cakes can I have?	A Any. B Three. C No-one.	B

16   Can I go out tonight?

    A   No, you can't.
    B   Tomorrow.
    C   At 10 o'clock.

17   What time's lunch?

    A   Tomorrow.
    B   At 1 o'clock.
    C   Two hours.

18   Do you want me to lay the table?

    A   That's good.
    B   No, you don't.
    C   Yes, please.

19   When will Dad be home?

    A   Yesterday.
    B   3 hours.
    C   Soon.

20   Where's the dog?

    A   Into the garden.
    B   Yes, he is.
    C   In the garden.

Questions 21 – 25

Complete the conversation.
For questions 21 – 25, mark the correct letter (A – H).

EXAMPLE		ANSWER
0 Mum:	Where are you, David?	G
David:	0............	

Mum: Where are you going on Saturday night?

David: 21.....C......

Mum: Is it near home?

David: 22...D....

Mum: What time does it finish?

David: 23....B.....

Mum: That's very late.

David: 24....F.....

Mum: OK, but you must do all your homework on Saturday.

David: 25...E.....

A   That's very late

B   About 2 o'clock in the morning.

C   To the concert. Is that OK?

D   Yes. It's next to our school.

E   I will. Thanks Mum.

F   Please, Mum. You have to let me go Everyone's going.

G   I'm here, in the kitchen.

H   No, you aren't.

Part 4
Questions 26 – 32

Read the letter that David has written to his friend in Spain.
Are sentences 26 – 32 'Right'? (A) or 'Wrong'? (B).

If there is not enough information to answer 'Right(A) or 'Wrong' (B),
choose 'Doesn't Say' (C).

For questions 26 – 32, mark A, B or C.

David Richardson is fifteen years old and he lives with his family in Manchester.
This is a copy of a letter he wrote to his new pen-pal in Spain.

Dear Juan,

Hello! My name's David and I'm fifteen years old. My birthday is on the thirteenth of March. My mother's name is Christine and she works part-time as a nurse. My father's name is Ted and he works full-time as a company representative. I've got two sisters; one is called Sarah and she's in her last year at school, and the other is called Jenny and she's very naughty. Sarah is seventeen and she's got a boyfriend called John. Jenny is only ten and she always annoys me when I'm studying.

We live in a semi-detached house with a little garden and we have a beautiful cat called Simon. I like playing with my cat but I don't like helping in the garden. Do you live in a house or a flat? Have you got any brothers and sisters? Do both your parents work?

In my next letter I'll tell you about my school.

Write soon.

David

26   David's birthday is on 30th March. B

A   Right   B   Wrong   C   Doesn't say

27   His mother works full-time. B

A   Right   B   Wrong   C   Doesn't say

28   Sarah is older than David.   C

A   Right   B   Wrong   C   Doesn't say

29   His father owns a company.

A   Right   B   Wrong   C   Doesn't say

30   They have a small garden. B

A   Right   B   Wrong   C   Doesn't say

31   Juan's parents both work. A

A   Right   B   Wrong   C   Doesn't say

32   David tells Juan about his school. B

A   Right   B   Wrong   C   Doesn't say

Read the article about Life in Britain.
Choose the best word (A, B or C) for each space (33 – 40).
For questions 33 – 40 mark, A, B or C.

·······LIFE IN BRITAIN·······

Britain has (Example: *some*) customs which are different from other countries, for example, did you know that in Britain most people have __33__ milk delivered __34__ their homes early every morning. __35__ night they put their __36__ milk bottles outside __37__ doors and in the morning the milkman takes the empty milk bottles away and leaves full ones in their place.

You __38__ buy your milk in the supermarket or local shop, if you prefer, but a lot of people __39__ like to have it delivered. The only problem is that __40__ little birds drink some of the milk if you don't cover the bottles or get up very early.

EXAMPLE			ANSWER
0 A Some	B A	C Any	A

33   A   his   B   its   C   their

34   A   at   B   to   C   in

35   A   At   B   In   C   On

36   A   full   B   empty   C   tall

37   A   our   B   his   C   their

38   A   must   B   can   C   have

39   A   yet   B   already   C   still

40   A   sometimes   B   ever   C   when

Part 6
Questions 41 – 50

Complete the following notes.
Write ONE word for each space (41 – 50).

Dear Michael

I (Example: <u>am</u>) sorry I didn't see <u>41</u> yesterday. We're
going swimming today <u>42</u> four o'clock. Do you <u>43</u>
to come? We <u>44</u> meeting outside the pool.
Bring <u>45</u> money.

See you

David

Dear David,

I <u>46</u> go swimming today. I <u>47</u> got to finish my
homework. I went <u>48</u> the cinema last night so I
must do <u>49</u> today.
Have <u>50</u> good time!

Michael

Part 7
Questions 51 – 55

Read this information about a boy who wants to send away for a T-shirt.
Fill in the information on the ORDER FORM.

> David Smith is 12 years old and he lives at 17, Windsor
> Park, Belfast BT9 6FR. His telephone number is 660502.
> He goes to Windsor Park School.
> He is very tall and a bit fat. He would like a red T-shirt.

ORDER FORM

First Name:		David
Surname:	51	
Address:	52	
Postal Code:	53	
Small/Medium/Large:	54	
Colour:	55	

You must meet your friend, Peter, after school today.
Write a note to him.

Say:

    <u>why</u> you want to see him
    <u>where</u> and <u>when</u> to meet you.

Write 20 – 25 words.

LISTENING PAPER

Part 1
Questions 1 – 5

Listen to the tape.
You will hear five short conversations.
You will hear each conversation twice.
There is one question for each conversation.
For questions 1 – 5, put a tick ✓ under the right answer.

Here is an example:

EXAMPLE

What time is the meeting?

20.30   **20.00**   **21.30**

A ☐   B ☐   C ☐

---

1   What time is it?

08.15   **08.50**   **07.45**

A ☐   B ☐   C ☐

2   What does Michael have for breakfast?

Orange Juice   Tea and Toast   Orange Juice
and Toast   and Cornflakes

A ☐   B ☐   C ☐

3   How much money does Michael need?

15p   **50p**   **5p**

A ☐   B ☐   C ☐

4   When is the school concert?

Tuesday   Thursday   Today

A ☐   B ☐   C ☐

5   When is Mary's party?

February 4   February 14   February 5

A. ☐   B ☐   C ☐

Part 2
Questions 6 – 10

Listen to Nicholas and Lucy talking about their families.
What have each of them got?
For questions 6 – 10, write a letter (A – H) next to each person.
You will hear the conversation twice.

EXAMPLE	ANSWER
0 Alan	E

PEOPLE

6   Lucy ☐

7   Nicholas ☐

8   Simon ☐

9   Nicholas' sister ☐

10   Nicholas' brother-in-law ☐

RELATIVES, ETC

A   Two brothers

B   Two sisters

C   No brothers or sisters

D   A boyfriend

E   A girlfriend

F   A nephew and niece

G   Two children

H   A dog

Part 3
Questions 11 – 15

Listen to Michael talking on the phone to a friend about a trip to see his relatives.
For questions 11 – 15, tick ☑ A, B or C.
You will hear the conversation twice.

EXAMPLE	ANSWER	
0 Michael is going to see	A a friend	☐
	B his cousins	☑
	C his brother	☐

11	Michael is travelling by	A car	☐
		B plane	☐
		C train	☐

12	The journey takes	A 6 hours	☐
		B 8 hours	☐
		C a lot of things	☐

13	He will be met by his	A uncle	☐
		B aunt	☐
		C cousins	☐

14	The weather will be	A dry	☐
		B sunny	☐
		C rainy	☐

15	Michael is going to take	A an umbrella	☐
		B warm clothes	☐
		C a raincoat	☐

Part 4
Questions 16 – 20

Listen to Sarah speaking on the telephone. She wants to speak to Olive, but she is not there.

For questions 16 – 20, complete the message to Olive.
You will hear the conversation twice.

MESSAGE

To:	(0)	**Olive**
From:	(16)	_____
Date:	(17)	_____
Time:	(18)	_____
Church:	(19)	_____
Hotel:	(20)	_____

Part 5
Questions 21 – 25

Listen to some information about an adventure park.
For questions 21 – 25, complete the message about the adventure park.
You will hear the information twice.

ADVENTURE WORLD

Opens:	9.00 am
Closes in winter:	(21) _____
in summer:	(22) _____
Cost for adults:	£8.00
for children:	(23) _____
Young children must be with:	(24) _____
For some rides you must be over:	(25) _____

TEST 2   SCHOOL

READING AND WRITING PAPER

Part 1
Questions 1 – 5

Who are these signs for?
For questions 1 – 5, mark A, B or C.

EXAMPLE		ANSWER
0 Please don't write on desks	A people B teachers C pupils	C

1 SILENCE PLEASE

A   students in a library

B   students in a classroom

C   people in a bookshop

2 Take off your shoes

A   students in the corridor

B   students in the class

C   students in the gym

3 No running in playground

A   car drivers

B   teachers

C   students

4 Turn off the taps, please

A   students

B   teachers

C   everybody

5 Assembly starts at 9.00am

A   the staff

B   everybody

C   the headmaster

Questions 6 – 10

Which notice (A – H) says this (6 – 10)?
For questions 6 – 10, mark the correct letter (A–H).

EXAMPLE	ANSWER
0 Exams start on Monday	D

6 You can have additional help when normal classes are over. *B*

7 There will be an excursion tomorrow. *C*

8 There is a meeting for the teachers tonight. *H*

9 There is a meeting for mothers & fathers this evening. *A*

10 On Friday you have to give back all books. *G*

A **Parents' meeting this evening at 8.00 pm**

B *Extra classes after school*

C **School trip tomorrow**

D Exams begin next week

E The books will be in the bookshop on Friday

F **YOU MUST GIVE YOUR NAMES FOR THE EXCURSION TOMORROW**

G **Please return all books to the library on Friday**

H **Staff meeting at 8 o'clock this evening**

Part 2
Questions 11 – 15

Read the descriptions (11 – 15) of some places in a school.
What is the name of each place (A – H)?
For questions 11 – 15, mark the correct letter (A – H).

EXAMPLE	ANSWER
0 Teachers meet here.	E

11   You can buy your books here.

12   You can read books here.

13   You can eat your school lunch here.

14   You can do P.E. here.

15   You meet here in the morning.

ROOMS

A   gym

B   classroom

C   bookshop

D   canteen

E   staff room

F   library

G   kitchen

H   assembly hall

Part 3
Questions 16 – 20

Complete the five conversations.
For questions 16 – 20, mark A, B or C.

EXAMPLE		ANSWER
0 Have I got an English lesson tomorrow?	A Yes, I have. B No, you aren't. C Yes, you have.	C

16   Have we got any homework?

    A   Yes, you are.
    B   No, there aren't.
    C   Yes, you have.

17   What time does the exam begin?

    A   Last night.
    B   At 9 o'clock
    C   Two days ago.

18   Can you lend me a pencil?

    A   Yes, I do.
    B   Yes, I can.
    C   No, I don't.

19   Is there a football match on Saturday?

    A   No, it isn't.
    B   Yes, it is.
    C   Yes, there is.

20   Where are the notebooks?

    A   Into the cupboard
    B   Onto my desk
    C   On my desk

Questions 21 – 25

Complete the conversation.
What does David say to Simon?
For questions 21 – 25, mark the correct letter (A – H).

EXAMPLE		ANSWER
Simon:	Have you done your Latin homework?	B
David:	0...........	

Simon: Neither have I why don't we do it together?

David: 21....E.....

Simon: Shall I come to your house or will you come to mine?

David: 22.....A.....

Simon: You live behind the school playground, don't you?

David: 23....G.....

Simon: Well, I'll come to your house at 10.00 in the morning.

David: 24.....F.....

Simon: OK. I'll come at 11.00.

David: 25....H.....

A   I don't mind.

B   Not yet. What about you?

C   Neither have I.

D   You don't mind.

E   That's a good idea.

F   That's very early.

G   Yes, that's right.

H   That's fine see you tomorrow.

Part 4
Questions 26 – 32

Read the letter David has written to his friend Juan about his school.
Are sentences 26 – 32 'Right' (A) or 'wrong' (B)?

If there is not enough information to answer 'Right' (A) or 'Wrong' (B),
choose 'Doesn't say' (C).

For questions 26 – 32, mark A, B, or C.

Dear Juan,

Our school is called Highfield and it has got 420 pupils, boys and girls. It's the biggest school in Oxford and I think it's the best. It's a comprehensive school so you don't have to pay school fees like you do in the private or "public" schools. (Yes, it's unusual that the top private schools in England are called "public" schools and some foreigners study at them. There are two very famous ones called Eton and Harrow).

As it is such a large school we have wonderful facilities: tennis courts, football pitches, an indoor heated swimming pool, hockey pitches and a snooker room. We also have a good canteen, a language laboratory where I practise my Spanish and French and a modern science laboratory.

We begin school at 9 o'clock in the morning and finish at 3.30 in the afternoon. We only have one hour for lunch which we have in the canteen. A few pupils prefer to bring a packed lunch. After school there are lots of activities such as stamp collecting, chess, theatre etc. In my next letter I'll tell you about my hobbies.
Write soon.

David

P.S. I forgot to tell you my favourite subjects. I prefer languages (I do French, Spanish, English and a little Russian) but I also like history, geography, art and P.E. I don't like chemistry or physics and I hate mathematics. What about you?

26   Highfield is the largest school in Oxford.

A   Right   B   Wrong   C   Doesn't Say

27   You have to pay to go to Highfield.

A   Right   B   Wrong   C   Doesn't Say

28   Public schools are free.

A   Right   B   Wrong   C   Doesn't Say

29   The school has an outdoor swimming pool.

A   Right   B   Wrong   C   Doesn't Say

30   Most pupils eat in the school canteen.

A   Right   B   Wrong   C   Doesn't Say

31   David likes stamp collecting and chess.

A   Right   B   Wrong   C   Doesn't Say

32   David will tell Juan about his hobbies the next time he writes.

A   Right   B   Wrong   C   Doesn't Say

Part 5
Questions 33 – 40

Read the article about life in England.
Choose the best word (A, B or C) for each space (33 – 40).
For questions 33 – 40, mark A, B or C.

•••••• LIFE IN ENGLAND ••••••

In Britain most children start nursery school when they are 3 years 0 . After this they begin primary school which they go to 33 they are 11. Children 34 go to State primary schools then usually go to secondary schools. You must stay 35 school until you are 16 when you do some important exams, called GCSE's.

If you do well in 36 exams you 37 continue for another 2 years specialising in three or four 38 . For example, English, French and German 39 Maths, Physics and Chemistry. Then you do more exams called A Levels and if your 40 are good you can go to University.

EXAMPLE			ANSWER
0 A old	B young	C age	A

33	A from	B since	C till
34	A which	B who	C what
35	A at	B on	C into
36	A these	B this	C that
37	A can't	B can	C have
38	A themes	B materials	C subjects
39	A and	B or	C with
40	A marks	B notes	C figures

Part 6
Questions 41 – 50

Complete these letters.
Write one word for each space (41 – 50).

Dear Mr Cooper,

I (Example: **am**) sorry I cannot come __41__ class today. I __42__ to stay __43__ home for a week because I have got the flu. I hope to be back at school on Monday.
__44__ you send me __45__ homework, please?.

Yours,

Sarah

Dear Sarah,

Thank you for __46__ note. I hope you get better __47__ .
If you want to do some exercises you can __48__ the one in your book __49__ page nine.
I hope to see you in class __50__ week.
    Yours,
            Mr Cooper

Part 7
Questions 51 – 55

Mark Smith wants to go on the school trip.
Read this information about him and then fill in the form the school gave him.

Mark Smith is 14 years old. He was born on the second of March 1979. He's in class nine. He has some problems with asthma and he is allergic to dust.

APPLICATION FORM

First Name:		Mark
Surname:	51	
Date of Birth:	52	
Class:	53	
Any Health Problems:	54	
Any Allergies:	55	

Part 8
Question 56

You will be late home from school today. Your mother is at work.
Write a note to her.

Say:

    <u>why</u> you will be late.
    <u>what</u> you will be doing and <u>when</u> you will be home.

Write 20 – 25 words.

LISTENING PAPER

Part 1
Questions 1 – 5

Listen to the tape
You will hear five short conversations.
You will hear each conversation twice.
There is one question for each conversation.
For questions 1 – 5, put a tick ✓ under the right answer.

Here is an example:

```
EXAMPLE

0     Which class do they have to go to?

2B                2V                2P
A  ✓            B  ☐            C  ☐
```

1   What time does the Spanish class begin?

9.15   **9.45**   **8.15**
A ☐   B ☐   C ☐

2   How long does the class last?

One hour   3/4 hour   1 hour 1/4
A ☐   B ☐   C ☐

3   When is the Spanish exam?

5th March   **15th March**   **5th May**
A ☐   B ☐   C ☐

4   Which page does the teacher say?

150   130   113
A ☐   B ☐   C ☐

5   Where does the teacher ask John to go?

To the teachers   To the room   To the teachers'
                                              room

A ☐   B ☐   C ☐

Part 2
Questions 6 – 10

Listen to Tim phoning to ask about their homework.
Tim asked Lucy six questions.
What did he ask Lucy about each subject?

For questions 6 – 10, write a letter (A – H) next to each subject.
You will hear the conversation twice.

EXAMPLE	ANSWER
0 Latin	B

SUBJECT

6 Biology ☐

7 Maths ☐

8 English ☐

9 History ☐

10 French ☐

QUESTION

A What exercises?

B What page?

C What number?

D What chapters?

E Title of composition

F What units?

G What vocabulary?

H What notebook?

Part 3
Questions 11 – 15

Listen to Jane telling Toby what happened in Latin class.

For questions 11 – 15 tick A, B or C.
You will hear the conversation twice.

EXAMPLE	ANSWER	
0 Mike arrived late for	A school.	☐
	B today.	☐
	C Latin class.	✓

11 Mr Spencer sent Mike	A out.	☐
	B home.	☐
	C away.	☐

12 Mike said	A he was late.	☐
	B he was sorry.	☐
	C he was on time.	☐

13 Mike's father is	A away.	☐
	B at home.	☐
	C out.	☐

14 Mr Spencer never listens to	A students.	☐
	B pupils.	☐
	C excuses.	☐

15 Jane will speak to Mr Spencer	A at lunch time.	☐
	B at break time.	☐
	C in the class.	☐

Part 4
Questions 16 – 20

Listen to a girl speaking on the telephone.
She wants to speak to Brian but he is not there.

For questions 16 – 20, complete the message to Brian.
You will hear the conversation twice.

MESSAGE

To: **Brian**

From: (16) _____

To go to: (17) _____

At: (18) _____

Bring: (19) _____

Stay for: (20) _____

Part 5
Questions 21 – 25

Listen to some information about a school.
For questions 21 – 25, complete the information about the school.
You will hear the message twice.

LITTLEFIELD SCHOOL

Closed until: 16 August

Office open from: (21) _____

In the morning to: (22) _____

Tuesday 17th meeting for: (23) _____

Thursday for: (24) _____

New pupils have to come on: (25) _____

TEST 3   HOME TOWN

READING AND WRITING PAPER

Part 1
Questions 1 – 5

Who are these notices for?
For questions 1 – 5, mark A, B or C.

EXAMPLE		ANSWER
0 **NO STOPPING**	A people B pedestrians C drivers	C

1   **NO PARKING**

A   drivers /
B   pedestrians
C   conductors

2   **CITY CENTRE STRAIGHT AHEAD**

A   campers
B   drivers
C   shop assistants

3   **CAR PARK FULL**

A   children
B   car owners
C   runners

4   **DON'T CROSS**

A   lorry drivers
B   drivers
C   pedestrians

5   **NO LEFT TURN**

A   children
B   shoppers
C   drivers

Questions 6 – 10

Which notice (A – H) says this (6 – 10)?
For questions 6 – 10, mark the correct letter (A – H).

EXAMPLE	ANSWER
0 You can buy stamps here	G

6   If you need urgent treatment go here.

7   You can ask for a map of the town here.

8   You can buy lottery tickets here.

9   We don't close for lunch.

10   If you see an accident go here.

A   **Museum open 9am to 5pm**

B   *LOTTERY TICKETS ON SALE HERE*

C   Tourist Information

D   **EMERGENCIES ONLY**

E   **HOSPITAL ENTRANCE**

F   **Police Station**

G   **Post Office**

H   **WINNING LOTTERY TICKET SOLD HERE**

Part 2
Questions 11 – 15

Read the descriptions (11 – 15) of some places.
What is the name of each place (A – H)?
For questions 11 – 15, mark the correct letter (A – H).

EXAMPLE	ANSWER
0 You can buy food here.	F

11   You can get tourist
     information here.

12   You can study here when
     you are eighteen.

13   You can buy nearly
     everything here.

14   If you want to borrow books,
     you go here.

15   You can see interesting
     old things here.

PLACES

A   shopping centre

B   museum

C   university

D   town hall

E   book shop

F   supermarket

G   library

H   secondary school

Part 3
Questions 16 – 20

Complete the five conversations.
For questions 16 – 20, mark A, B or C.

EXAMPLE		ANSWER
0 Do you need any stamps?	A Yes, I have. B Yes, I do. C No, I needn't.	B

16 What time does the museum open?
    A Since 9 o'clock.
    B At 9 o'clock.
    C 9 hours.

17 Where is the nearest church?
    A Yes, of course.
    B Two hours.
    C I don't know.

18 Are there many Chinese restaurants in Oxford?
    A Yes, much.
    B Yes, a lot.
    C Yes, a little.

19 What is Oxford most famous for?
    A His boat race.
    B Her street.
    C Its university.

20 Is it far to the town centre?
    A Not very.
    B A lot.
    C Far away.

Questions 21 – 25

Complete the conversation?
What does Jenny say to Mary?
For questions 21 – 25, mark the correct letter (A – H).

EXAMPLE		ANSWER
Jenny:	Can you answer some questions about Oxford University?	D
Mary	0............	

Jenny: How old is Oxford university?

Mary: 21...................

Jenny: How many colleges has it got?

Mary: 22...................

Jenny: Can anyone go to it?

Mary: 23...................

Jenny: How long do you have to study to get your degree?

Mary: 24...................

Jenny: It's a beautiful university. I would love to go there.

Mary: 25...................

Jenny: Because I don't think I'm intelligent enough!

A   It depends on your notes.

B   3 or 4 years.

C   I don't know.

D   Yes, of course I can.

E   Why don't you?

F   Yes, if they get excellent marks.

G   It's beautiful, isn't it?

H   About 800 years old.

Read the article about a girl from Barcelona.
Are sentences 26 – 32 'Right' (A) or 'Wrong' (B).

If there is not enough information to answer 'Right' (A) or 'Wrong' (B), choose 'Doesn't say' (C).

For questions 26 – 32, mark A, B or C.

I LOVE ENGLISH!

Yolanda Pérez is just 15 years old. This summer she is studying English in Oxford. This is what she told our interviewer.

What do you think of Oxford?
Well, I think it's fantastic. There are many beautiful buildings, the parks, the river, the university...

Is there anything else you especially like about it?
Yes, the wonderful atmosphere in the streets with so many tourists and students from all over the world. There are also lots of interesting museums to visit and plenty of sports facilities.

What do you not like about Oxford?
Most people say the weather but because I am only here for July and August I don't mind a little rain and some cloudy days. In my country it's too hot in August.

Where are you staying in Oxford?
I'm staying with a very nice family. I must say the food is much nicer than I thought it would be.

Do you like learning English?
I love learning English. I want to be an English teacher when I am older. But now I must go - my next class starts in five minutes.

26 Yolanda likes the atmosphere in Oxford.

A Right   B Wrong   C Doesn't say

27 There are few sports facilities.

A Right   B Wrong   C Doesn't say

28 Yolanda thought the food would be better.

A Right   B Wrong   C Doesn't say

29 Yolanda likes pubs a lot.

A Right   B Wrong   C Doesn't say

30 Yolanda doesn't mind the English climate in summer.

A Right   B Wrong   C Doesn't say

31 Yolanda is an English teacher.

A Right   B Wrong   C Doesn't say

32 Her next class begins soon.

A Right   B Wrong   C Doesn't say

Read the article about an English town.
Choose the best word (A, B or C) for each space (33 – 40).

·····AN ENGLISH TOWN·····

In an English town or village most people live in houses ___0___ a garden. The average family ___33___ got two children and the mother and father usually ___34___ work. A lot of families ___35___ have a cat or a dog. The town usually has post offices, schools, banks, churches, cinemas, restaurants, discos, pubs etc. It also ___36___ a police station, a town hall and a hospital.

English pubs are ___37___ all over the world. They are not just ___38___ because you can eat in them, play snooker or darts, listen to music and so on. In short, you ___39___ have a very good ___40___ there.

EXAMPLE			ANSWER
0 A in	B with	C from	B

33	A has	B is	C are
34	A two	B both	C the two
35	A also	B too	C to
36	A does	B has	C is
37	A visit	B famous	C in
38	A bars	B a drink	C for drink
39	A do	B can	C have
40	A funny	B enjoy	C time

Part 6
Questions 41 – 50

Complete these letters.
Write one word for each space (41 – 50).

Dear Nigel,

We're having a scout meeting (Example: **in**) the church hall
___41___ afternoon.   It will begin ___42___ four o'clock and
___43___ about seven o'clock.   If you ___44___ come please
leave a message for me.

See you ___45___.

Yours,

John Smith

Dear Scout Master,

Thank ___46___ for your note.   I am very ___47___ but I can't
___48___ to the meeting this afternoon.   I have a very difficult
exam ___49___ Monday morning and my mother says I
___50___ to study.

I'll see you at church tomorrow.

Yours

Nigel Brown

Read the information about a family who want to vote.
Fill in the information on the census card.

Jonathan Cowling is from London. He's nearly 39.
He's single and he lives at 266, St Margaret's Road,
Twickenham, London.

CENSUS CARD

First Name: Jonathan

Surname: | 51 |

Sex: | 52 |

Age: | 53 |

Full address: | 54 |

Marital status: | 55 |
(single/married)

Part 8
Question 56

You want to go to the cinema with a friend. Leave a note for him.

Say:

   <u>what</u> film you want to see.

   <u>where</u> and <u>when</u> to meet you.

Write 20 – 25 words.

LISTENING PAPER

Part 1
Questions 1 – 5

Listen to the tape.
You will hear five short conversations.
You will hear each conversation twice.
There is one question for each conversation.
For questions 1 – 5, put a tick ✓ under the right answer.

Here is an example:

EXAMPLE

0 What time does the post office open?

0830	**0900**	**0930**
A ☐	B ☐	C ✓

---

1 How much does a lottery ticket cost?

£1.50	**£1.00**	**£1.15**
A ☐	B ☐	C ☐

2 When is the film on?

Tuesday 4th	Thursday 14th	Tuesday 14th
A ☐	B ☐	C ☐

3 Where is the police station?

Behind the town hall	**Next to the town hall**	**Opposite the town hall**
A ☐	B ☐	C ☐

4 How many books can you borrow from the library?

3 times a week	3 every 2 weeks	2 every 3 weeks
A ☐	B ☐	C ☐

5 Which church does the girl go to?

St Mary's	St Paul's	Opposite St Paul's
A ☐	B ☐	C ☐

Part 2
Questions 6 – 10

Listen to Lucy talking to Rachel about her shopping trip.
Lucy went to six shops.
What did she buy in each shop?

For questions 6 – 10, write a letter (A – H) next to each shop.
You will hear the conversation twice.

EXAMPLE	ANSWER
0 Supermarket	B

	SHOP				THINGS BOUGHT
6	Off licence	☐		A	Champagne
				B	Groceries
7	Boutique	☐		C	Jeans
8	Garden centre	☐		D	Dress
				E	Plant
9	Record shop	☐		F	Flowers
10	Toy shop	☐		G	Doll
				H	Compact disc

Part 3
Questions 11 – 15

Listen to David talking the hospital receptionist and then to his friend Michael.
For questions 11 – 15, tick ✓ A, B or C.
You will hear the conversation twice.

EXAMPLE	ANSWER	
0 The patient's name is	A Michael Curran.	✓
	B Michael Curren.	☐
	C Michael Currin.	☐

11   Michael is on

- A   the second floor.   ☐
- B   the second ward.   ☐
- C   the men's floor.   ☐

12   Michael broke his leg playing

- A   basketball.   ☐
- B   American football.   ☐
- C   football.   ☐

13   Michael will be in hospital for

- A   two weeks.   ☐
- B   two months.   ☐
- C   two days.   ☐

14   The nurses are

- A   not so bad.   ☐
- B   not very good.   ☐
- C   very nice.   ☐

15   David is going to bring him

- A   some biscuits and a drink.   ☐
- B   fruit and biscuits.   ☐
- C   Some fruit and a cake.   ☐

Part 4
Questions 16 – 20

Listen to a girl called Susanna reporting a robbery to the police.

For questions 16 – 20, fill in the crime report.
You will hear the conversation twice.

CRIME REPORT

Name: _Susanna_

Surname: (16) _____

Robbed at: (17) _____

        in: (18) _____

        by: (19) _____

Handbag contained purse,
make-up and: (20) _____

Part 5
Questions 21 – 25

Listen to some information about a Science Museum.

For questions 21 – 25, complete the information about the Science Museum.
You will hear the message twice.

SCIENCE MUSEUM

Opens: _____9.00am_____

Closes: (21) _____

Cost for adults: (22) _____

For students and children: (23) _____

Special school trips on: (24) _____

Creche for children under: (25) _____

TEST 4 HOBBIES AND SPORTS

READING AND WRITING PAPER

Part 1
Questions 1 – 5

Who are these notices for?
For questions 1 – 5, mark A, B or C.

EXAMPLE		ANSWER
0 **You must change your shoes**	A people entering a gym B people playing table-tennis C people playing billiards	A

1 **Please return balls**   A

    A tennis players
    B swimmers
    C chess players

2 **YOU MUST WEAR A BATHING CAP**   B

    A golfers
    B swimmers
    C basketball players

3 **QUIET PLEASE**   C

    A football spectators
    B rugby spectators
    C tennis spectators

4 **MEMBERS ONLY**   C

    A people joining a club
    B people leaving a club
    C people entering a club

5 **Family changing rooms**

    A families who want to change rooms
    B people who want to change families
    C families who want to change together

A

Questions 6 – 10

Which notice (A – H) says this (6 – 10)?
For questions 6 – 10, mark the correct letter (A – H).

EXAMPLE	ANSWER
0 You can learn to dance in the afternoon	C

6   You can shop in a new sports shop soon.   *G*

7   Skis are cheaper now.   *B*

8   Our shop is open this afternoon.   *H*

9   If you want to go to the big match, come in!   *A*

10   At the moment all our products are cheaper.   *F*

A   **FOOTBALL TICKETS ON SALE HERE**

B   **BIG REDUCTIONS ON SKIS**

C   **BALLET CLASSES 3–6PM**

D   **CHEAPEST SPORTS SHOP IN TOWN**

E   **SKIS FOR HIRE**

F   **EVERYTHING REDUCED**

G   **SPORTS SHOP OPENING SOON**

H   **CLOSED FOR LUNCH 1–2 PM**

Part 2
Questions 11 – 15

Read the descriptions (11 – 15) of some places.
What is the name of each place (A – H)?
For questions 11 – 15, mark the correct letter (A – H).

EXAMPLE	ANSWER
0 You can skate here.	B

11   If you play tennis, you book one.

D

12   You play football here.

G

13   If you do athletics, you run here.

A

14   This is where you go to collect shells.

C

15   You do exercises to get fit here.

F

PLACES

A   track

B   ice rink

C   beach

D   pitch

E   camp

F   gym

G   court

H   race course

Part 3
Questions 16 – 20

Complete the five conversations.
For questions 16 – 20, mark A, B or C.

EXAMPLE		ANSWER
0 Do you like acting?	A Yes, I have. B No, I'm not. C Yes, I do.	C

16 Can you ride a horse?

A

A Yes, I can.
B No, I don't.
C Yes, I do.

17 Do you want to come cycling
with me on Saturday?

C

A Yes, please.
B On Saturday.
C Yes, I went.

18 How much do the tickets for
the football match cost?

B

A Very much.
B That's expensive.
C I don't know.

19 Are you playing hockey on
Sunday?

B

A That's all right.
B I hope so.
C I think I have.

20 When is the rugby match?

A In the rugby club.
B Last week.
C On Saturday.

Questions 21 – 25

Complete the conversation.
What does Richard say to Christian?
For questions 21 – 25, mark the correct letter (A – H).

EXAMPLE	ANSWER
Christian: Hi Richard, how are things?	B
Richard: 0............	

Christian: Fine. are you playing basketball on Saturday?

Richard: 21 ....

Christian: I'd like to go to watch you play with a friend

Richard: 22 ....

Christian: Where is the match? Is it at home?

Richard: 23 ....

Christian: What time do we have to leave?

Richard: 24 ....

Christian: That's very early. I'll have to go to bed early tonight.

Richard: 25 ....

Christian: Don't worry. I won't.

A   No, it's an away match.

B   OK, what about you?

C   Please don't be late.

D   The bus leaves at 6 in the morning.

E   Yes, of course I am.

F   That would be great.

G   The bus leaves at 3 in the afternoon.

H   Please come early.

Read the interview with a British P.E. teacher called Mr Brown.
Are sentences 26 – 32 'Right' (A) or 'Wrong' (B)?

If there is not enough information to answer 'Right' (A) or 'Wrong' (B),
choose 'Doesn't say' (C).

For questions 26 – 32, mark A, B or C.

What sports do you play at your school?
In winter we play rugby or football or go cross-country running. Some girls play netball or hockey and next year we hope to have a boy's hockey team too.

Do only boys play rugby or football?
No, we have a very good girls' football team and we've just started a girls' rugby team.

Is sport compulsory in British schools?
Yes, you have to play sport at least one afternoon a week, but you don't have to take a sports exam, as you do in some countries for example, Spain.

What sports do you play in summer?
The boys play cricket but I'm sure it won't be long until the girls play too. Boys and girls go swimming, do athletics and girls play rounders which is similar to baseball. We also have tennis courts.

Is sport a popular subject?
Yes, very. Much more than before because everyone is health conscious now and wants to get fit. The only thing I don't like about being a sports teacher is that the younger children never want to have a shower!

EXAMPLE	ANSWER
0 They don't play rugby or football in summer	A
A Right B Wrong C Doesn't say	

26   Only boys play rugby at Mr Brown's school.

A   Right   B Wrong   C Doesn't say

27   Some boys play hockey.

A   Right   B Wrong   C Doesn't say

28   The girls' rugby team is very good.

A   Right   B Wrong   C Doesn't say

29   Sport is compulsory in British schools.

A   Right   B Wrong   C Doesn't say

30   The pupils have to do a sports exam.

A   Right   B Wrong   C Doesn't say

31   There is a girls' cricket team.

A   Right   B Wrong   C Doesn't say

32   The younger children don't like having a shower.

A   Right   B Wrong   C Doesn't say

Part 5
Questions 33 – 40

Read the article about cricket.
Choose the best word (A, B or C) for each space (33 – 40).
For questions 33 – 40, mark A, B or C.

CRICKET

Most people know there is a sport called cricket __0__ they don't understand how it is played.   This is not surprising! Cricket is a very complicated sport.

There are eleven __33__ on each team and they all __34__ white clothes. They play with two bats and a ball.   One of the strangest things __35__ cricket is that the match can go on all day or __36__ for five days! It is played in summer in England and it is a very typical sight to see families in pretty villages __37__ cricket played __38__ grass.

Cricket began in England but it is also very popular __39__ India, Pakistan, the West Indies, Australia and New Zealand.

People get very passionate about cricket in __40__ countries but the rest of the world thinks it's very boring!

EXAMPLE			ANSWER
0 A but	B and	C or	A

33 A players   B games   C teams

34 A dress   B carry   C wear

35 A about   B on   C over

36 A during   B even   C including

37 A watching   B looking   C watching at

38 A over   B on   C above

39 A at   B in   C into

40 A this   B that   C these

Part 6
Questions 41 – 50

Complete these letters.
Write one word for each space (41 – 50).

Dear Min,

I (Example: **am**) sorry I can't wait __41__ you any longer.
I __42__ to go to the doctor. If you __43__ I can play tennis
with you tomorrow __44__ .

__45__ you book the court?

Thanks,

Mary

Dear Mary,

I'm __46__ I arrived late yesterday. I have booked __47__
court for 3 o'clock. Is that __48__ ? Can you bring an extra
racket __49__ mine is broken?

See you __50__

Min

Read this information about a family who want to join a sports club.
Fill in the information on the application form.

Mr and Mrs Richardson have got two daughters and one son. Mr and Mrs Richardson both play squash and tennis. Their son likes table-tennis and swimming but their daughters don't like either tennis or swimming, they prefer gymnastics.

FAMILY APPLICATION FORM

Surname: Richardson

Number of children: | 51 |

Sports they are interested in:

Mr Richardson | 52 |

Mrs Richardson | 53 |

Their son: | 54 |

Their daughters: | 55 |

Part 8
Question 56

You want to go cycling with your friend, David, tomorrow morning.

Write a note to David.

Say:

where to meet you and at what time.

Also what he has to bring.

Write 20 – 25 words.

LISTENING PAPER

Part 1
Questions 1 – 5

Listen to the tape.
You will hear five short conversations.
You will hear each conversation twice.
There is one question for each conversation.
For questions 1 – 5, put a tick ✓ under the right answer.

Here is an example:

EXAMPLE

0 Which hockey stick does the boy want?

The red one   **The blue one**   **The red and blue one**

A ✓   B ☐   C ☐

---

1   What sports does the woman play?

golf and table-tennis   table-tennis   **tennis and golf**

A ☐   B ☐   C ☐

2   How much does the court cost per hour?

£1.30   **£1.50**   **£1.15**

A ☐   B ☐   C ☐

3   When is the handball match?

5th July   **6th July**   **4th July**

A ☐   B ☐   C ☐

4   Where is the squash club?

on the right   **on the left**   **in the centre**

A ☐   B ☐   C ☐

5   What time does the match begin?

3.30   **4.30**   **3.13**

A ☐   B ☐   C ☐

Part 2
Questions 6 – 10

Listen to William talking to Raymond about summer camp.
Here are six of the sports you can play.
What do you need for each of these sports?

For questions 6 – 10, write a letter (A – H) next to each sport.
You will hear the conversation twice.

EXAMPLE	ANSWER
0 Table-tennis	C

SPORT		**THINGS BOUGHT**
6 Tennis	☐	A Racquet
		B Horse
7 Hockey	☐	C Bat
8 Cycling	☐	D Stick
		E Mountain bikes
9 Handball	☐	F Motorbike
10 Riding	☐	G Swimming pool
		H Net

Part 3
Questions 11 – 15

Listen to Johnny taking to Paul about rugby.
For questions 11 – 15, tick ☑ A, B or C.
You will hear the conversation twice.

EXAMPLE	ANSWER	
0 The match is	A on the second.	☐
	B on Saturday.	☑
	C in a week.	☐

11	Paul now has to train	A 3 times a week.	☐
		B twice a week.	☐
		C for a week.	☐
12	The trainer is	A nice.	☐
		B friendly.	☐
		C unfriendly.	☐
13	If they win each player will get	A a medal.	☐
		B a cup.	☐
		C a medal and a cup.	☐
14	The match is against	A ANST.	☐
		B ENST.	☐
		C INST.	☐
15	Johnny's going to bring his	A camera.	☐
		B video camera.	☐
		C cassette recorder.	☐

Part 4
Questions 16 – 20

Listen to Charles talking to a friend's sister on the telephone.
He wants to talk to his friend but he is not there.

For questions 16 – 20, complete the message to Monica's brother.
You will hear the conversation twice.

MESSAGE

To:	(16) _____
From:	(17) _____
Taken by:	**Monica**
Meet Outside:	(18) _____
At:	(19) _____
Match is at:	(20) _____

Listen to some information about a sports club.

For questions 21 – 25, complete the information about the sports club.
You will hear the information twice.

SPORTS CLUB

Opens:		8 o'clock
Closes:	(21)	
Membership costs:	(22)	
Family membership costs:	(23)	
Price for Children (for One day):		£1
Members can bring one guest per:	(24)	
No visitors on:	(25)	

TEST 5   JOBS

READING AND WRITING PAPER

Part 1
Questions 1 – 5

Who are these notices for?
For questions 1 – 5, mark A, B or C.

EXAMPLE		ANSWER
0 **Change towels every day**	A waitresses B chefs C chambermaids	C

1   **Please type these letters**

    B   A   secretaries
         B   postmen
         C   lawyers

2   **GIVE TABLETS THREE TIMES A DAY**

    A   A   chemists
         B   nurses
         C   patients

3   **ALWAYS CHECK CUSTOMERS' CHANGE TWICE**

    A   A   shop assistants
         B   customers
         C   clients

4   **Never leave children's classes unattended**

    C   A   teachers
         B   professors
         C   students

5   **NOT MORE THAN THREE PASSENGERS**

         A   bus drivers
         B   taxi drivers
         C   train drivers

Questions 6 – 10

Which notice (A – H) says this (6 – 10)?
For questions 6 – 10, mark the correct letter (A – H).

6   You can get your hair done here.

_B_

7   We make furniture.

_F_

8   We work quickly.

_D_

9   You can get legal advice here.

_A_

10   We don't open in the morning.

_E_

A   **LAWYER'S OFFICE**

B   **Cut and blow dry £6.50**

C   **Best carpenter in town**

D   **Shoe repairs while you wait**

E   Office open 2pm–6pm

F   **EXPERT FURNITURE REPAIRS**

G   **Opening hours 8am – 12 noon**

H   **DRESSMAKERS**

Part 2
Questions 11 – 15

Read the descriptions (11 – 15) of people who need something or someone.
Where do they need to go (A – H)?
For questions 11 – 15, mark the correct letter (A – H).

EXAMPLE	ANSWER
0 If you need oil for your car you buy it here.	F

		PLACES
11	People with toothache go there. *D*	A garage
12	If you have a problem with your car you take it here. *A*	B barber's
13	You phone here if the central heating is broken. *E*	C carpenter's
14	If you feel ill you go there. *H*	D dentist's
15	Only men have their hair cut here. *G*	E electrician's
		F petrol station
		G hairdresser's
		H health centre

Part 3
Questions 16 – 20

Complete the five conversations.
For questions 16 – 20, mark A, B or C.

EXAMPLE		ANSWER
0 Is your work interesting?	A Not very. B A lot. C Yes, he is.	A

16   Where do you work?

    A   In an office.
    B   Next year.
    C   I don't know.

17   What would you like to be?

    A   I like being a doctor.
    B   Yes, I would.
    C   A journalist.

18   How long have you worked there?

    A   8 hours a day.
    B   For 3 years.
    C   2 miles.

19   How much do you earn?

    A   Yes, very much.
    B   A long time.
    C   £1000 a month.

20   Do you like your job?

    A   I'd like to be a singer.
    B   I like dancing.
    C   No, I don't.

Questions 21 – 25

Complete the conversation
What does Jim say to Anne?
For questions 21 – 25, mark the correct letter (A – H).

EXAMPLE		ANSWER
Anne:	Hi, I haven't seen you since you got your new job. How's it going?	C
Jim:	0............	

Anne:	What's wrong? You don't look very happy. Don't you like it?	A✓ The problem is the boss.
Jim:	21.....................	B No, actually I'm well paid.
Anne:	Is it a hard job? Do you have to work very long hours?	C✓ Well, it's going OK.
Jim:	22.....................	D He's awful. He shouts all day long.
Anne:	Is the pay bad then? Do you earn very little?.	E No, I win a lot of money.
Jim:	23....................	F I like him a lot.
Anne:	I don't understand. What is the problem then?	G✓ Yes, I do like it but ...
Jim:	24....................	H✓ No, it isn't the hours.
Anne:	Oh dear! I didn't think of that. What's he like?	
Jim:	25.....................	
Anne:	Poor Jim!	

Part 4
Questions 26 – 32

Read the interview with the careers teacher.
Are sentences 26 – 32 'Right' (A) or 'Wrong' (B)?

If there is not enough information to answer 'Right' (A) or 'Wrong' (B),
choose 'Doesn't say' (C).

For questions 26 – 32, mark A, B or C.

Do you think we will get a job when we finish university?
Well, I can't promise that but I can give you some useful advice.

What is the first thing we should do?
First of all write a really good curriculum vitae with all the necessary information about yourself. The school you went to; your work experience; your hobbies and interests. Include a photograph.

What else is important?
It's very important to have some work experience. During your summer holidays try to find a job. If you are studying tourism for example, try to get a summer job in a hotel. The experience of working is more important than how much money you earn.

What about interviews?
Of course it's very important to arrive punctually and look smart. However, this is not enough. You should do more than just answer questions, you should also ask some questions and show interest in the job.

Is that all we need to know?
No, I think there is one more very important thing. A lot of young people say they can't get a job but in fact what they mean is that they can't get a job in their own town or near their own town. You must be prepared to travel to work or even live away from home. It's much easier to get the job you want if you are already working.

Thank you very much for answering our questions.
Not at all. I've enjoyed talking to you. Good luck with your careers.

26   A C.V. is the information you write about yourself when you are looking for a job.

A   Right   B   Wrong   C   Doesn't say

27   It is important to earn a lot of money if you work

A   Right   B   Wrong   C   Doesn't say

28   It is more important to arrive on time for an interview than to be well dressed.

A   Right   B   Wrong   C   Doesn't say

29   During the interview you should only answer questions.

A   Right   B   Wrong   C   Doesn't say

30   You should only look for work near your home.

A   Right   B   Wrong   C   Doesn't say

31   If you have a job it is not so difficult to get another one.

A   Right   B   Wrong   C   Doesn't say

32   You should be prepared to live away from home.

A   Right   B   Wrong   C   Doesn't say

Read the article about work.
Choose the best word (A,B or C) for each space (33 – 40).
For questions 33 – 40, mark A, B or C.

━━━━━ WORK ━━━━━

Nowadays it is normal to work eight hours _0_ day in most countries of the world. You cannot work legally _33_ you are _34_ sixteen years old.

Earlier this century, however, the situation _35_ very different. Very young children _36_ very dangerous jobs. Children as young _37_ six years old worked in coalmines. People worked very long hours in extremely bad conditions and were very badly paid. Unfortunately, this _38_ happens in some countries.

The main problems today are that many people _39_ got a job and many _40_ work have to travel long distances to get there and so the working day is still very long.

EXAMPLE			ANSWER
0 A in	B a	C the	B

33	A until	B if	C unless
34	A under	B down	C for
35	A was	B were	C went
36	A did	B done	C made
37	A so	B as	C than
38	A yet	B even	C still
39	A haven't	B don't	C won't
40	A what	B who	C why

Part 6
Questions 41 – 50

Complete these letters.
Write one word for each space (41 – 50).

Dear Mr Matthews

I am (Example: **sorry**) I cannot come __41__ work this week.
I __42__ got a very bad backache. The doctor says I __43__
stay in bed __44__ a week.

If you __45__ me to do some work in bed please send me a
note. (I can't answer the telephone!)

Sorry,

Richard

Dear Richard

Don't worry. I don't want you to work __46__ bed, I want you
to __47__ better __48__.

I will come to see __49__ after work __50__ Wednesday.

Yours

Mr Matthews

Read this information about a man who is applying for an office job.
Fill in the information on the job application.

> Paul Topping is 20 years old and he is looking for a job in an office. He has worked in another office since he was 17. He is single. He likes his job but he would like to use computers more. He has done a course in them.

JOB APPLICATION

First Name:		Paul
Surname:	51	
Age:	52	
Marital status:	53	
Years of experience:	54	
Course/s in:	55	

Part 8
Question 56

You have got a new job.

Write a note to a friend.

Explain:

<u>what</u> the job is

<u>when</u> you have to start and <u>how much</u> you will earn.

Write 20 – 25 words

LISTENING PAPER

Part 1
Questions 1 – 5

Listen to the tape.
You will hear five short conversations.
You will hear each conversation twice.
There is one question for each conversation.
For questions 1 – 5, put a tick ✓ under the right answer.

Here is an example:

EXAMPLE

0 What time is it?

0745　　　　　**0645**　　　　　**0715**

A ✓　　　　　　B ☐　　　　　　C ☐

1　Where is Jane's office?

At the traffic lights　　　**On the left**　　　**Opposite the cinema**

A ☐　　　　　　　　　　B ☐　　　　　　　C ☐

2　When did Jane begin working there?

Two months ago　**In July**　　　　**In June**

A ☐　　　　　　　　　B ☐　　　　　　　C ☐

3　How much does Jane earn?

£850 a month　　　**£1,500 a month**　　**£1,050 a month**

A ☐　　　　　　　　B ☐　　　　　　　C ☐

4　What's the office like?

Large and new　　　**Big but old**　　　**Small but modern**

A ☐　　　　　　　　B ☐　　　　　　　C ☐

5　Where does Jane have lunch?

In a cafe　　　　　**In a bar**　　　　**In the office canteen**

A ☐　　　　　　　　B ☐　　　　　　　C ☐

Part 2
Questions 6 – 10

Listen to Sally talking to Lucy about what jobs she would or would not like to do.
Lucy talks about six jobs.
What does she need for each of these jobs?

For questions 6 – 10, write a letter (A – H) next to each job.
You will hear the conversation twice.

EXAMPLE	ANSWER
0 Office clerk	B

	JOB			WHAT YOU NEED
6	Bank clerk	C	A	experience
			B	typing and computer studies
7	Reporter		C	A levels
			D	G.C.S.Es
8	Air hostess		E	languages
			F	a degree
9	Teacher		G	teaching experience
10	Shop assistant	A	H	a degree and a diploma

Part 3
Questions 11 – 15

Listen to Miss James at a job interview.

For questions 11 – 15, tick ☑ A, B or C.
You will hear the conversation twice.

EXAMPLE	ANSWER	
0 Miss James can speak	A 5 foreign languages	☑
	B 3 foreign languages	☐
	C 2 foreign languages	☐

11	Her mother is	A English.	☐
		B Spanish.	☐
		C French.	☐
12	She learnt Russian	A at school.	☐
		B at university.	☐
		C in Russia.	☐
13	The hotel is called	A Montara.	☐
		B Montana.	☐
		C Montena.	☐
14	She worked there for	A 4 years.	☐
		B 4 summers.	☐
		C 4 months.	☐
15	She could begin work	A next week.	☐
		B after the interview.	☐
		C on Monday.	☐

Part 4
Questions 16 – 20

Listen to a girl speaking on the telephone.
She wants to speak to Paul, but he is not there.

For questions 16 – 20, complete the message to Paul.
You will hear the conversation twice.

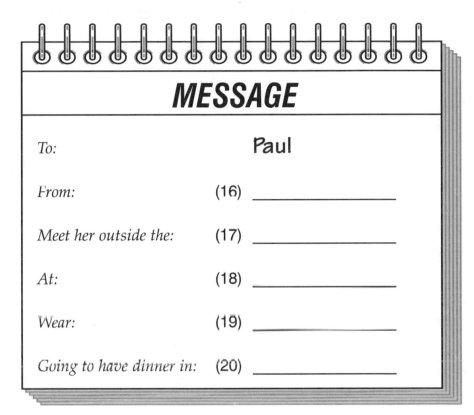

MESSAGE

To:	Paul
From:	(16) _____
Meet her outside the:	(17) _____
At:	(18) _____
Wear:	(19) _____
Going to have dinner in:	(20) _____

Listen to some information about evening classes.

For questions 21 – 25, complete the information about the evening classes.
You will hear the information twice.

EVENING CLASSES

Classes from: _7 p.m._

To: (21) _____

Students must be over: (22) _____

Spanish classes cost: (23) _____

Advanced computer courses
   on Tuesday and: (24) _____

Computer classes cost: _£75_____

Maximum number of students
   in French classes: (25) _____

THE LEARNING CENTRE
HAMMERSMITH AND WEST
LONDON COLLEGE
GLIDDON ROAD
LONDON W14 9BL
0181 741 1688